8 EZ Steps
to
Financial Success

8 EZ Steps to Financial Success

By
William Cristo Jr., MD, J.D.

E-BookTime, LLC
Montgomery, Alabama

8 EZ Steps to Financial Success

ISBN: 1-59824-304-7

First Edition
Published July 2006
E-BookTime, LLC
6598 Pumpkin Road
Montgomery, AL 36108
www.e-booktime.com

Contents

Introduction

The purpose of writing this book is to help you increase your wealth. The way to increase your wealth is to increase your assets. This is accomplished by not spending money foolishly. One should not overspend, but instead one should over save. How many of us have spent four dollars on a cup of coffee at Starbucks™ or some other fancy coffee shop. If one merely goes to a regular coffee shop or machine a coffee costs about one dollar. This will save you three dollars. If you multiply this by five days a week this comes to fifteen dollars a week. Multiply this by fifty weeks a year comes to seven-hundred and fifty dollars a year saved. This assuming you only have one cup of coffee a day. A second cup of coffee would merely increase the savings to about fifteen-hundred dollars per year. If one takes a normal work span of thirty years, this would save a total of approximately forty-five thousand dollars. Adding interest on would increase it enormously. Needless to say, this would save enough for a down payment for a house, a car, or contribute significantly toward a child's education.

This merely represents one example of how one can save oodles of money. It is not necessary to read the entire book at one sitting. It would be wise to merely scan the chapters and then read the appropriate sections as necessary.

Chapter I

General Comments

I was riding in the back of my Uncle Pete's brand new Cadillac in New York City when my Uncle told me that I had a thousand dollars extra in student loans for medical school. My response to my Uncle was "should I send the thousand dollars back". He said, "hell no, let's invest it". Hence, an investor was born. He subsequently invested it in a paint company earning 8 to 12 percent interest per year. This was a significant amount of cash for me as a student and helped me learn the basics of investing.

I then went on to buy small amounts of stock in Johnson & Johnson, Comp™, GE™, and various other companies appeared. Over the past twenty-five years, this has significantly raised my net worth. I would like to note that I never ever was able to put in ten thousand dollars or so until recently. In the beginning, I merely invested a thousand dollars at a time. That's the secret. Increasing your assets is best performed by slowly adding money over time.

Indeed, one philosopher, whose name I cannot think of right now, suggested that the best way to increase money was to give it some time to earn interest.

Please note I am not talking about a large sum. A small amount will do. For example, how many of us receive small rebates for buying various items in the range of $10, $15, $25. If these were merely saved, bundled up and cashed in at one time, the reward would be enormous. All one has to do is put them in a special bank account in bunches and eventually as you approach one-thousand dollars then decide what to do with the money. This is exactly what I have done over the past twenty, twenty-five years. If you do the same you will also succeed. Remember there is no instant formula to accumulating significant wealth.

Over time, of course as time moves on and you accumulate more and more wealth you will be able to invest it in larger amounts. This is indeed what I have done. Starting with that thousand dollars from the student loan, I have been able to reinvest, reinvest and reinvest.

It also helps to live slightly beneath your means. As a physician, people always ask me why don't I have a bigger house, why don't I have three cars in the driveway, why don't I have a BMW™? The answer is live slightly beneath your means. I do have a Cadillac and I have had about five Cadillac's during my professional career. However, I have either leased them at zero percent interest, paid for them at zero percent interest, or leased and then purchased them to get the best price. After all, a Cadillac is still a Cadillac. I would never go to a foreign car as they are much too expensive to repair and too expensive for routine maintenance. For example, I routinely go to Firestone or Goodyear where an oil change is approximately fifteen dollars and sometimes ten dollars. Many times once you apply for a Goodyear or Firestone credit card, coupons are mailed to you for cheaper oil changes including low prices for alignment, tire change, etc. I repeatedly take advantage of these offers as per manufacturer's suggestion.

Chapter II

Step 1 - Foundation

How many times have you gone by a construction site where they are building a home, a factory or a condominium? You probably will note the first thing they dig holes. Second thing is a solid cement platform followed by sides of concrete blocks, cement or other such materials. In addition, there is evidence of rods, metallic rods, inside the cement. These rods provide a stronger foundation. Without these rods, the building could collapse during times of stress in the foundation or the ground.

In a similar matter, one must supply a solid foundation for a savings or investment program to proceed ahead. In this case, a solid foundation merely means $500 to a $1,000, not large amounts of concrete blocks, cement and/or rods. How then does one achieve this?

The answer is very simple. One must build a foundation much like one is building a building. In our case the foundation means a small amount of cash or MONEY. Now, how does one accumulate a collection of cash to start an investment plan and build a firm foundation? If I didn't know the answer, I wouldn't ask the question. The answer is quite simple. Most of us work on a salary with a certain amount paid per day, per week per month or for a period of time. Almost all of us receive excess cash in one form or another. For example, do you ever work overtime? If you do, there is extra money. Do you ever have a small side job? If you do, there is also extra money. Do you ever get Internal Revenue Service rebates or rebates from the State that you live in around tax time? If you do, there is extra money. I myself started with a thousand dollars left over from a student loan. I was riding in the back of my rich Uncle's Cadillac and asked, "Uncle Pete, should I return the thousand dollars to the bank, as I will be in excessive debt when I finish college?" He said, "hell no, let's invest it." He invested it in a paint company that paid approximately 10-12% a year or about 1% a month. Hence, an investor was born.

Also, do you receive money on your birthday? Do you receive any rebates? Most of us receive rebates from dentists, doctors, products you bought, etc. There is one case where I purchased a computer and received a check for a hundred dollars about a month later. By that time I had forgotten about the hundred dollars and this certainly could have been used for investment purposes to build up my collection of cash, or a thousand dollars to start with.

Besides, has anyone of you ever kept track of the money you spent foolishly? There is a young lady who works with my wife at Boston College. She routinely spends $4 a day on a "Starbucks"™ coffee. I am thoroughly amazed by this as I, as a physician, go to the coffee machine in the hospital, or the hospital cafeteria and buy a seventy-five cent or one-dollar cup of coffee. If this young lady does this every day, which she does, she is wasting twenty-dollars a week, or approximately one-thousand dollars a year. Over a twenty year working career this would amount to approximately twenty-thousand dollars. With interest, dividends, etc., this I am sure would amount to approximately thirty to forty thousand dollars which would be a fantastic amount for a down payment for a house.

In summary then, treat any extra cash that you have as an "internal dividend". Use this to build up your collection of money for a good foundation for your retirement plan or your savings plan.

A good first step might be to include such small checks into a savings account and slowly build it up to $500 to $1,000. Add to it periodically as you can, and I am sure you will be quite happy with the results.

Remember, even small amounts add up. I have a small piggy bank which I drop quarters, nickels and dimes into almost everyday. I suspect it contains about $200-$300 worth of money.

Of course, one need not return bottles at five cents a piece in order to build up a thousand dollars worth of equity. Just take these small steps that I mention and I am sure you will succeed.

Chapter III

Step 2 - Budget

One again we all live on a paycheck whether it be daily, weekly, monthly or quarterly. If you do put in some overtime this results in excess cash. If you perform a side job this also results in excess cash.

The first step then is to form a budget for yourself and your family. I routinely make up a budget approximately once a year. Every month I try to assess how much I need for rent, for operation of my car, for food and clothing, etc. If these figures are off, I merely correct them after two or three months. Of course I stay within my budget of the amount of money I make every month.

As extra checks come in, whether they are dividends, interest payments, etc., they are shuttled directly to a savings account.

Now comes the difficult part. As November approaches, we will also notice a decrease in Social Security payments, Federal and State tax payments. Hence, your take home pay will be greater. The trick here is to keep your take home pay the same and save the increased money that hence you did not know you had. This then gives you a bonus for approximately six to eight weeks toward the end of each year. Do not spend this money. This should be added to your savings account, which you started earlier. Once again, any extra checks whether they are rebates, check returns from doctors, dental bills, etc., should also all be added to the savings account. Just pretend they don't exist and sign them over to your savings account.

Unlike my wife's friend, don't spend four-dollars a day on a cup of coffee. Spend a dollar.

Further, many people waste five to six dollars on lunch money, I see it routinely. One could always bring a sandwich and a dessert to work and buy a cup of coffee or buy a soda. This would save you $3 to $4 a day, which could subsequently be saved on a weekly or bi-weekly basis. Now I don't encourage you to live as a hermit, but try to save whatever you can. If you feel you must buy lunch, try buying it maybe once a week or once every two weeks. But certainly do not buy a complete lunch every single day as it becomes much more expensive than the previously mentioned cup of coffee.

In addition, look around you to consider other ways to save money. If you drive a car and park at the office, is the parking free? If it's not free, as it is not in Boston, you might consider parking in a different lot where the rate might be somewhat cheaper. This would also save a lot of money.

If it is cheaper to take a subway or bus line, please do so. It also is certainly cheaper to buy the tickets every month even though you don't go in every single day. This would also save on transportation costs and any residual funds could be saved to the savings account.

As a married man, my wife loves to go out to eat. Hence, we go out to eat approximately once a week. If you are a businessperson, you probably can deduct some of these dinners if you discuss business. The only requirement of the I.R.S. is that business be discussed during the dinner. Any money saved from taking some of these dinners during the year could also be saved into your savings account.

If you merely think clearly for about a week or two, you probably will find enormous places where you can save $5, $10 or $15 here or there. Again, I am not talking about five cents on a Coca Cola™ bottle that is to be returned. I'm talking about significant amounts of money, which can be added to your foundation in the savings account.

As this foundation builds up, then we should consider how to invest the money. One might consider investing it temporarily in a one-year CD or some other such vehicle where the interest rate is slightly higher. But always keep in mind that money might be used for a house, a car, a future wedding ceremony, college tuition, etc. Please remember not to leave the money in too long as you may want to invest it in stocks or bonds or other investment vehicles that yield significantly more than the bank.

Chapter IV

Step 3 - House Rent

As I eluded previously, I used to pay approximately eleven-hundred dollars a month rent. I subsequently purchased a house across the street from where I used to rent. My full criteria was that the house payment be no more than the rent payment. This house payment includes, of course, principal, interest, taxes and insurance. Hence the new house payment had to be approximately what the old rent payment was. Why am I so stringent about this? Because as my income goes up, the most expensive part of my day or month, namely mortgage payment, will always be the same. It will of course increase slightly with taxes. However, as the income goes up this eleven-hundred dollars a month stays the same and I can subsequently save the difference. If one is a renter, try to get a reasonable rental close to where you work. Naturally, one would try to get a lease of some duration where the rent will be fixed for two to three to four years. Always retain an opt out clause in the lease where if you find a house at a good value you can opt out of the lease with reasonable notice.

Further, some homes will rent with an option to buy. In the Boston area, where rentals run approximately $2,000 a month, many landlords might be willing to give you, let us say 10% of the rental value toward the down payment. If the rent were $2,000 a month or $24,000 a year, you would be able to put $2,400 toward a possible future purchase of the property, whether it be a condominium or a full house. Also, as you live your life wherever you are, look around your neighborhood. I frequently took walks around the block and visualized other places that were being sold or people who had passed away. Many times the relatives want to sell the house quite quickly after a death and therefore will settle for a lower price. Indeed, I purchased my current property at a significant discount from retail price with no 6% brokerage fee. How did I do this? Very simple, by putting up a significant down payment, I believe it was $40-60,000 from savings. Further, I guaranteed that there will be no problem obtaining a mortgage. Needless to say, I saved several thousand dollars on the closing cost. The house has since tripled in value.

In summary, live in a reasonable rent district, keep your eyes open, keep saving money and try to avoid excessive Realtor fees if possible. This also might be achieved by looking at the Sunday paper. There are many, many houses for sale by owner where the realtor's fee does not exist and the person is merely interested in selling quite quickly due to a death in the family or other unforeseen circumstances. Please remember, one can always take advantage of these situations and save a lot of money.

Now, what about maintenance on a house or rental unit? On a rental unit the answer is obvious; it is a landlord's responsibility. On a house, the answer is also obvious, it's your problem. As you walk around the neighborhood and meet your neighbors try to talk to the elderly. They frequently have invaluable contacts with work-men who they have known for years. I did this quite by accident and found men who replaced the windows in my home, replaced the siding on my home and did various other jobs well, well, well below the normal retail price. Sometimes one must compromise and the men do the work on Saturdays, evenings or some holidays. Who cares? The fact is, my siding was put on beautifully, my windows were put in beautifully, and other areas, including kitchen and bath, were also redone during the evenings. One fellow even started the job, then went hunting for two or three months and then finished the job. Who cares? If one is single, or married without children, it is quite easy to delay a job a few months and save lots and lots of money.

Chapter V

Step 4 - A Car

When considering the purchase of a car or a pickup truck or some other means of transportation, one must ponder the following questions:

1) Is a car necessary?

2) Can I achieve the same objective by using public transportation? After all public transportation is cheap and frequently gives discounts especially when purchased on a monthly basis.

3) If I decide not to buy a car and use public transportation, can I rent a car by the day when necessary? There are many companies out there that are more than willing to lease cars by the day, by the week or by the month. If you do this frequently, once or twice a month, they will certainly give discounts. This is frequently a way to have a vehicle in a large city and yet not have the expense of parking, insurance, etc.

4) Should the car be new, brand-spanking new, or slightly used? Here the answer is somewhat difficult but I will attempt to apply principles that I have learned over 30 years.

A new car will frequently cost very close to list price. If you wait for sales, Washington's Birthday, etc. the price will be subsequently reduced. It will be further reduced if one waits until the end of the model year; however, the car will be almost a year old. Further, there are many, many sales inducing one to buy at 0% interest, 1.9% interest, etc. One should peruse these very carefully. As to complicate matters further, one is frequently asked to decide between a low percent interest rate or a $1,000 or $2,000 rebate. This depends on your individual situation. If your credit is in good shape you should take the 0% interest and pay over two to three years. Because after one or two years you will probably get small raises which will make the car payment somewhat easier to absorb.

One should also consider the miles per gallon of a vehicle. This is very important. I remember my first car got 8 miles per gallon. My current car gets 24 miles per gallon. Sure the price of a gallon of oil has increased quite a bit but I am saving a bit by having the car run three times more efficiently.

In addition, one must always consider the guarantee for a car. I prefer bumper-to-bumper warranties for four years with a maximum of 50,000 miles. This has saved my neck and wallet many many times. Frequently one can purchase a guarantee. Consumer Reports™ advises that it's not worth a guarantee. However, with today's complicated vehicles it frequently is.

I once had a Cadillac that was approximately 9 years old worth about $4,000. The check engine light kept coming on. No one could find anything wrong with it. After approximately $1,000 I thought the problem was fixed. However, as I went to sell the car the check engine light came on once again. Needless to say these problems can drive one to the insane asylum. On a nine-year-old car, I don't think the advice is to get a guarantee, however, for the new car, at a four-year guarantee, or possibly purchasing a four-year guarantee for a few thousand dollars, it might be worth it. Once again it's an individual call. If possible, it might be possible to delay the purchase of extended warranty after the original warranty runs out. This would give a person the chance to assess the vehicle, see how it runs, if it leaks oil, etc., etc., etc. Therefore, one could have some idea if the car was worth the extra one or two thousand dollars for an extended warranty or not. Again, it's an individual call. Keep reading magazines such as Consumer Reports™, Consumer's Digest™, etc. for evaluations. Also, please note in these magazines whether the car has been recalled. Many times cars have been recalled with various problems which should have been covered by manufacture's warranty. There are many hidden recalls which are not publicized until the customer comes in with a problem.

In any case, try to get the most miles per gallon out of a vehicle. Almost every weekend New York Times™, and various other newspaper and magazines have summaries of cars and their performance. Also, if you go to Edmunds.com on the web, there are frequently surveys of the best cars, the most efficient cars, etc.

Having said that, the next question is, should one lease a car? Almost every accountant I have ever spoken to agrees that it is much much more expense to lease than to buy. Further, they all agree that when you lease a car you can deduct part of the expenses. I frequently challenged them and asked them the question can I also deduct it when I buy it? The answer is yes, you can deduct the depreciation, gas and oil expenses, maintenance expenses, etc. Hence, the value of leasing a car comes out marginal at best. In addition, many studies in Consumer Reports™, Consumer's Digest™ and other magazines have shown that the difference is within 5% and hence negligible.

However, if you do decide to lease, remember these words, CAPITALIZED COST REDUCTION. This is a number which represents a dollar figure that you must pay when you lease the car. This is non-refundable and non-returnable. This is a down-payment which tends to reduce the monthly payments. However, it comes directly out of your pocket when you lease a car. Hence, it is not desirable to lease a car with a capitalized cost reduction as it frequently runs into thousands of dollars.

If capital cost reduction amounts to zero or a dollar, it might be wise to look into the offer further. However, one must also realize that there is a leasing rate. The first car I leased years ago was given to me with a lease rate of 0%. This would be highly desirable meaning there is no interest charges. However, one must look very carefully for other charges such as charges when the car is returned.

Charges for knicks and dents, and tires, etc. I know of one physician who had a three-year-old BMW and returned it at the end of the lease period. Somehow charges for the return of the car amounted to something in the neighborhood of $3,000 in addition to his capitalized cost reduction charges. If you like throwing money in the trash this is ideal situation. If you don't, avoid this.

Having said that, there is one way which might be acceptable to lease a car. If there is no capitalized cost reduction, payments are low due to 0% interest, etc. However, please always check the buy-out figure at the end of the lease. In other words, what can you buy the car for at the end of the lease? In this way, you do not have to have a down payment. You merely make the payments. At the end of the lease then you buy the car at a reasonable figure. The problem is what is a reasonable figure in three years for a new car?

This can be obtained by consulting Edmunds.com and various other used car websites to see what a three-year-old car in the category that you are looking at is worth. One could also check E-Bay™ and see what a three year old vehicle is worth. However, this is past history and may not represent the future price of your car. Indeed, one must search very carefully and do lots of homework before one decides to lease.

How about purchasing a car at the end of someone else's lease? This seems like a positive approach. The car is usually two or three years old. The dealer will usually guarantee it for another one or two years. And, believe it or not, it is usually about half the price of a new car. Further, many dealers check the car for defects at the end of the lease and you are buying virtually a 100% guaranteed car which has been thoroughly inspected from bumper to bumper. This indeed probably represents a good deal. Indeed, I have met many people including one Real Estate broker who purchased a car off lease. In every case I have looked at the car very carefully and it looks virtually new due to the excellent maintenance given a leased car, the excellent inspection at the end of the lease, and the beautiful body work or polishing done when the car is offered for sale. Remember, this car has been basically sold twice, once to the lessee and once to you, so try to get the dealer down as low as possible. If the dealer does not come down much in price ask him to pay for maintenance for one or two years or extended warranty for three more years. Get the idea? If you can't get the cash at least get a guarantee of free maintenance, free routine services, etc. for a long period of time. They usually will bite on a deal like this. There is another possibility. A friend of mine did this. This is going to a local gas station in your neighborhood asking him/her if he knows of a small dealer who sells cars in the range of $1,000-$4,000. My friend did such a thing and found a lovely car that was about eight years old for $3,000. She has had the car for about three years with not a problem. Further, when she has a minor problem, she goes to the dealer right a way and he corrects it since he was responsible for the car in the first place, and wishes to maintain his reputation.

Insurance

No discussion about purchasing a car can be complete without a discussion of insuring the vehicle. The answer to this is also somewhat complicated. However, there are several basic rules one should follow:

1) Shop for the highest deductible you can afford. As a striving student, I had a $1000 deductible, now I have $500 deductible. As one accumulates wealth during one's lifetime it is easy to keep $500 in a separate account just for the event of an automobile accident. This could be used at that time. Meanwhile you are paying much less in insurance premiums.

2) Shop around very carefully, check with all insurance companies. The airways, TV stations and radio stations are frequently flooded with advertisements. Shop around carefully and get the best quote.

3) Always ask if there is a discount? Many times discounts are present but they are not advertised. Students receive discounts. People with disabilities receive discounts. Senior Citizens

receive discounts. And surprising enough, people who do not drive much also receive a discount. In summary, don't forget to ask for a discount.

Repairs of the vehicle

As we've said up above, it is wisest to buy a car with a long-term guarantee, whether it be off lease or new. However, inevitably there are problems. Tires, oil changes, etc. frequently must be performed on a routine basis. The manufacture will stress that this should be done at their dealership. Frequently there is a tremendous markup at the dealership. Hence, I would advise that repair work be routinely done elsewhere. If it's a problem involving the guarantee, one could then return to the dealership for the appropriate repairs. I have done this at least ten times in my career.

Now in terms of general repairs, oil changes, etc., it is frequently much cheaper to go to Firestone™, Goodyear™, etc. Why? Because they frequently mail you coupons for discounts on oil changes and other routine maintenance items such as transmission fluid changes, etc. However, do not be sucked in with windshield wiper changes. Do that yourself and save $20 for repair. The advantage of these credit cards, Firestone™, Goodyear™, etc. is that frequently when a big repair is necessary, they will give you three month grace to pay the bill, and by grace I mean zero interest charges during the three month period. For example, I recently had a bill for about $400 for various items that had to be changed including a tire and alignment, etc. However, I asked the dealer at Firestone™, would this be eligible for the three month payment, he said, of course yes. That means I merely have to pay $125 a month for the next three months rather than $375 up front. Also, this is a good way of building up your credit report by showing that you can actually make the payments on time for three or four months. Further, if you decide to apply for a credit card from one of these dealers, frequently the oil change is free. They do this as an attempt to build new customers. Since I have had a Firestone™ credit car since 1989, I would say this is quite a successful approach.

Parking

Parking is always a problem in any city that I know. Hopefully, parking is included with your job. If it is not, look for the cheapest parking possibilities in the neighborhood. Remember, its always good exercise to walk a few minutes to and from your car at the beginning and end of the day. This helps your cardio-vascular system and keeps you in good shape. Hence, it might be wise to pay a little bit less and park a little bit farther away.

I frequently know people in Boston who park the car in the suburbs and take the T-line into Boston with a monthly pass. Although this sounds complicated it really is not and it usually is much cheaper than paying to park downtown at the rate of $20 plus per day. I am frequently horrified when I do have to go in, park downtown and pay $14 to see a doctor for about one hour. This is more than the deductible on the insurance plan. Hence, please think carefully where you park your car and stay open to all possibilities.

In summary, I would like to stress the following points:

- Leasing should be a last resort. My technician once said "Leasing is for Losers"

- Leasing costs more than buying

- If you buy you can still deduct mileage or percent of expenses if it is used for business purposes

The following are examples of practical ideas as of March 2005. These may change so do your research carefully.

- Some leases require $0.00 as a down payment. Check these out if you must lease. Also check out the re-sale price (the price YOU must pay to buy the car at the end of the lease). Example... Kia requires no down payment.

- Once in a while, at the end of a model year, you can obtain a better lease deal.... Remember $0.00 down.

- **Don't** pay a "Capitalized Cost Reduction" Fee

- Tis better to buy and hold than to lease. You have nothing at the end of the lease but an option to buy a car at a certain price.

- You are responsible for every little dent at the end of a lease. I know a Doctor who paid $3,500 at the end of a lease for dents, tires and repainting two panels on the car, a BMW of course. He could have purchased the tires and fixed the dents and saved at least $2,000.

Chapter VI

Step 5 - Credit Cards

Benjamin Franklin said "neither a lender or a borrower be," however in today's society it is frequently necessary to borrow money. For example, in the previous chapter we discussed borrowing for a large car repair when the payment could be made over three months with hopefully no interest. In addition there are frequently events when you have to borrow to buy something in the $500 - $1,000 range or higher. This is optionally done with a credit card as long as you have the means to pay it back within the required period of time. Normally two to three weeks.

Therefore, it is important that you obtain a good credit history and look for a cheap credit card. Ten, fifteen years ago one used to pay $25 a year for the privilege of dealing with various credit card companies. However, today, there is no charge for credit cards. Indeed, some such as the Sony™ card give you a $100 credit on opening an account. Others give you 5% or 1% back depending on your purchase. These are wise choices as this gives you an opportunity to build up your savings. One credit card limits itself to a $250 rebate per year. However, utilizing the $100 Sony™ card as well as the Citibank™ 5% card, one could build up $350 very quickly in the period of several months. As the amounts approach $50 or more one is able to cash the check in and apply into your savings account, thus building up your net wealth. After all, this is why you are reading my book, isn't it?

In summary, the following points apply:

1) Do not pay for credit card.

2) Find the cheapest interest rate credit card.

3) Try to find a credit card with a rebate such as the Sony™ credit card with a $100 rebate.

4) Try to find credit cards with 1% or 5% rebates on monthly basis and save the money in your savings account.

I would be negligent not to mention that you must never ever be late with a credit card payment. This involves extra fees, extra charges and extra money which you do not need to spend. Therefore, be careful and pay your credit card bills on time even if you have to starve for a day or two.

In this regard I would like to give an example of American Express™ credit card. There is no APR rate for 6 months. After that it becomes 10%. However, should you miss one payment the APR becomes 18%. Should you miss two or more payments the APR becomes 21.99%. In addition, the first six months of zero interest is waived. Hence, you can see once again why it is so important to pay the credit card bill on time even if you have to skip a meal in a restaurant or go out one less time per month with your friends.

Chapter VII

Step 6 - Bank and CD's

The first thing I would encourage anyone to do is open up a common regular plain old vanilla savings account. This will be your base for future investment.

The next step is to decide how much you can afford to save per week. Let's assume you start with ten dollars a week. Try this out for several months and see how you do. In addition, if you receive checks for birthday, Christmas, rebate or other reasons please deposit these into the account. The objective is to get this account to approximately one-thousand dollars. I realize interest rates are very low at the time of this writing, but the prime objective is to get it up to one-thousand dollars.

As you keep on saving whether it's that money from the Starbucks^{TM} cup of coffee or other vehicles, please deposit the money into the account. As you approach amounts over a thousand dollars, it is time to start thinking about CD's.

CD's are merely certificates of deposit. You must leave the money in the bank for a certain period of time during which they will guarantee you a certain interest rate. These come in various flavors such as one year CD's, two year CD's, five year CD's, etc. Normally, you would not bother with these until you have well over a thousand dollars.

Assuming you do, it would be wise to invest the first thousand dollars into a CD.

The next question is how long a CD should I buy? The answer is quite variable. If you are buying a house within the next one to two years you want a short CD. If you are buying a car within the next one, two, three years you want a short-lived CD. If you are not planning to buy a house for several years you might want a long CD such as a five-year CD. Remember, as the length of the CD increases, so does the interest. The problem is interest rates go up and your CD rate stays the same. This is where the banks have you trapped.

As you approach two thousand or more dollars it might be wise to ladder the CD's. The way to do this is to put, for example, one-thousand dollars in a one-year CD, the second thousand dollars might be in a three-year CD. A third three-thousand dollars might be in a five-year CD. Indeed, my wife has a friend at Massachusetts Institute Technology™ who does exactly that.

What is the rational for buying multiple rate CD's with multiple time periods? The answer is that the CD's mature at different times. For example the one year CD will mature in one-year. At that point, it can be reinvested hopefully at a higher rate. The three-year CD matures two years after that. That also could be invested hopefully at a higher rate. The five-year CD would also be hopefully reinvested at a higher rate. This assumes that interest rates are going up. Because had you invested all the money in a five year CD at the low rate, you might be crying if interest rates go up and you are not getting your fair share interest rate for the period of time.

As you all know, checking accounts are no longer paying interest. I have made several hundred dollars on checking account interest over the years. However, unfortunately, this era is over.

Whatever you do, do not commit yourself for an excessive period of time with a CD. Remember, ladder the CD's. This involves one year, three year, five year, etc. Also, always look for the bank with the highest CD. Why? Because money is spongeable. It is all the same. It matters not. If you go to Bank of America™, Chase Manhattan Bank™, or CitiBank™. You still get the same government guarantee.

In fact, if you are computer literate, it might be wise to go on the Internet and see what other banks are available. There is a bank called Orange Bank™. This pays a reasonable rate of interest which appears to always be higher than the local banks. Why is this you ask? Because, the Internet banks have no need for physical offices every five or ten blocks in the city, hence they can pay more to their depositors.

Also, if you are fortunate enough to be employed by an entity such as the government, labor union, or other organization that has a credit union, feel free to check out these rates. Frequently, credit union rates are also somewhat higher than a local bank but not high as an Internet bank.

In any case, make sure you are insured in the bank. Even if the bank goes bankrupt you will get your money plus interest to the date of the bankruptcy.

The objective here, of course, is to build up your capital for future investment, whether it be a car, a house, a wedding, a child's education or whatever you desire. This is indeed the most convenient way to build up capital and build up interest. Remember, the power of compounding is amazing. Unfortunately, you must pay tax on the interest as it accrues. Many states including Massachusetts frequently tax interest from a bank at a much lower rate.

In any case, this is probably the best way to slowly accumulate capital and triple your wealth. Indeed, my wife's friend has at least sixty to eighty thousand dollars in CD's. I frequently criticize her for not investing in other things. However, she feels CD is as safe as a rock, solid as gold and government guaranteed. She is, of course, correct. Furthermore, she plans on buying a second condominium near the Boston area and selling her first condominium. Since the first condominium is now paid for, the money that is in her CD's would be added to the first condominium's profit, thus enabling her to pay cash for the second condominium and have no mortgage payment. This is a situation which everyone dreams about. When you only have to pay taxes and insurance—no mortgage payment whatsoever.

In summary:

1) Try to build up your cash well over a thousand dollars.

2) As you build up thousand dollar increments start investing in CD's of various time lengths.

3) Reinvest in the CD's as they accrue with interest.

4) Always keep your eye on your objective, whether it be a house, a car, a wedding, or a child's education. Frequently ask yourself am I getting the maximum return for my dollar invested?

Chapter VIII

Step 7 - Bonds

What is a bond? A bond is a promise of a corporation, government entity or other organization to pay you interest after a certain period of time. In other words, the company, government entity or other organization is loaning you money for fixed period of time with a promise to return it along with interest. Interest could be paid monthly, quarterly, bi-annually, or annually. The problem is bonds come in units of five-thousand dollars or more. For the beginning investor, it is very difficult to build up five-thousand dollars.

Hence, an entity was formulated called a Bond Fund. This is a conglomeration of bonds managed by someone for a small fee which performs a similar function but lets you start with a thousand dollars or less depending on the company running the fund. In the case of accounts for students or children, you frequently can start with one-hundred dollars a month, if you promise to invest a hundred dollars a month on a monthly basis from your checking account. These are very good deals if the company is reliable such as Fidelity ™, VanGuard™ or Price™. Always look for the lowest charges on the types of funds that you wish.

There are really several types of funds. However, as a beginner one should be concerned with a reasonable yield or possibly a yield which is federal tax free and state tax-free. If you live in New Hampshire or Florida or Texas, there is no state tax and one only need be concerned with federal tax free funds.

In any case, I have dealt with funds for years and years and years; I find this a very useful vehicle in order to pursue your dream, whether it is a car, a house, or a child's education. It can also help triple your wealth. Whether or not you want a car, a house, or subsidize a child's wedding, or college education.

Feel free to use sources such as Money Magazine™, Smart Magazine™ and other magazines to assess bond funds. They frequently describe bond funds as well as stock funds in great detail and have comparisons amongst the various funds giving you some idea of what you can expect. They also mention several CD rates which also gives you some sort of idea of what you can expect on your money. In summary, the following points should be addressed:

1) Look for a bond fund which does not charge many fees.

2) Look for a bond fund with a decent yield.

3) If you can, try to get a tax-free bond fund that simplifies your taxes at the end of the year.

4) Many funds will let you start with a lower amount of money if you promise to invest fifty to a hundred dollars a month. This is indeed a good deal and you will be surprised how fast the money multiplies with the interest.

5) Try to credit the interest every month rather than take it as cash. This again will significantly increase your net worth.

Don't forget, as you increase your net worth you are then able to buy a house with a reasonable down payment, a car or start saving for a child's education.

I stress these three points because this is your ultimate objective, isn't it? When you triple your wealth, you are able to afford a house, a car, or a child's college education. Believe me, there is no greater satisfaction than being able to pay cash for certain items or put down such a large down payment that they give you the absolute minimum interest rate for the item that you are purchasing.

Chapter IX

Step 8 - Stocks and Investments

Many patients have asked me the following questions:

1) What is a stock?

2) What is the stock market?

3) Can I lose money on the stock market?

4) Can I lose all my money on the stock market?

5) Can I make money on the stock market?

The object of this chapter is to answer some of these questions. Let us stick with the first question. What is a stock? A stock is basically a share of a company or an entity. Companies may have a hundred shares of stock or ten million shares of stock. By buying one share or a hundred shares you own a proportionate share of that company.

Think of it as a pie. The pie can easily cut into eight slices. If you take one slice you own one-eighth of the pie or approximately 12%. If the pie has twenty slices and you take one slice you own 5% of the pie. Most people own only one or two-hundred shares perhaps a thousand shares of a company. Hence, they own a small piece of the pie. In most cases the pie amounts to millions of shares.

Hence, you own a relatively small portion of the company. For example, if you own a hundred shares out often million shares you own one one-hundred thousandth of a company which is a relatively small percentage. However, the stock is freely tradable and does declare dividends. It also may go up or down in value.

What is the stock market? The stock market is really multiple locations in New York, Boston, L.A., etc. where the stocks are traded daily. People phone their brokers or agents and buy or sell during normal business hours. Naturally, the price can go up or it can go down. The trick is to buy low and sell high. Invaluable research can be obtained on the Internet by typing the name of the company into Yahoo or Google and research stock prices back as many years as you wish. However, this is a topic for another book.

Can you lose money in the stock market? The answer is absolutely positively yes. There are many foolish people who invest thousands of dollars and lose it in a day. Therefore, one must be extremely careful how one invests. It also helps to do considerable research on a company before buying it. However, the most successful investment where one does not lose money is where the purchase was made and the stock was held for many years.

Can you lose all your money? The answer is absolutely unequivocally yes. If you invest all your money in one entity such as Enron™ or other companies which have gone bankrupt in the last several years you can lose your entire investment as well as your entire retirement account. Therefore, it pays to diversify. This means buying different companies. Never, never, never invest all your money with one company. In other words, if your company has an investment stock plan in a certain company, fine, however, always put money in other companies, not just one company. If that company should go bankrupt you will wind up with absolutely nothing.

This brings us to question number five. Can I make money in the stock market? The answer is absolutely positively yes. Many historians have noted that the stock market has gone up an average of 10.7% per year since 1926. This encompasses a period of time of approximately 80 years. However, certain years such as in the depression and during wartime, the market may temporarily go down. Other people have studied ten-year blocks since 1926. The results truly are astounding. Once again, 10.7% for your return, however, no one has ever lost money over a ten-year period since 1926. This is indeed the type of investment one would like to have. The catch is you must keep the money at least ten years.

There is a rule called the rule of seventy-twos. Take seventy-two divide it by the return, in this case 10.7% or approximately 11%, and you get a number of 6.73. This means your money will double in approximately 6.7 years. Should you keep the money, twice that amount or 13.4 years, you will have quadrupled your money with very little if any effort.

This then is the theme of the book, how to triple your net wealth.

So the idea on its simplest basis is to invest money and basically leave it in for long periods of time. This virtually guarantees that it will double or quadruple over 6.7 or 13.4 years respectively.

Now, of course, one cannot start with five dollars. Therefore, I encourage initial savings to be in a savings account despite the low interest. One can only invest in the market after one has saved a substantial amount of money such as one thousand, two-thousand or five-thousand dollars. Indeed, if you walk into a broker with twenty dollars he would probably laugh at you.

Next question is, how adverse am I to risk? There are basically three categories of investors: Conservative, middle of the road, and aggressive. I myself am a middle of the road/conservative investor.

A conservative investor researches the company very carefully on the Internet, finds out how long the company has been in existence. He checks dividends, he checks charts, and he checks stock prices, etc. and decides the company is very careful, considerate with his cash and does not take much risk. Examples of such a company would be General Electric or Johnson & Johnson.

An aggressive investor would pursue companies such as Enron or other entities which questionable nature, and have questionable stock performance and have questionable earnings. These are very risky stocks and usually one loses money.

Therefore, a good choice is the middle of the road where one proceeds with caution, studies the companies and perhaps buys one-hundred or two-hundred shares of stock at a time instead of purchasing an entire block on one day.

Now that we have covered the basic definitions, one should realize that it is very easy to start with only a thousand dollars that one has built up in a savings account. There is a book entitled "Buying Stocks Without a Broker" by Charles Carlson. This book and others like it, describe every Dividend Reinvestment Plan (DRIP) existing in the United States.

A DRIP plan is a plan where one starts with a small amount of money, perhaps a thousand dollars. Then, as dividends build up, they are automatically reinvested i.e., dividends are reinvested in the plan and buying you more stock. Mr. Carlson's book details some one-hundred pages of stocks as well as slight histories on each company.

For example, on page 90 he describes SBC Communications, formerly Southwestern Bell. He describes it as one of the seven spin offs of AT&T and describes it in three or four paragraphs. He also comes up with a conclusion as to what he thinks will happen over the next several years with the company. Remember of course this is just his opinion.

At the back of the book on the last one-hundred pages he describes further how one can get started in an SBC or South-western Bell Communications DRIP plan. He describes specifics, including a phone number to call, when dividends are paid, how much can be put in every month, etc. By the way, he gives SBC a five-start rating which is fairly high. Remember, this is just his opinion. Please check other opinions. However, the point is you can save on a monthly basis.

For example, when you do build up your one-thousand dollars and you consider SBC or any other company, you merely call the 800 number in the book which happens to be 1-800-351-7221 and ask for a prospectus. You then study this prospectus and the accompanying forms. If you wish you can fill out the forms with a check for a thousand dollars. As you wish you can reinvest money and have your dividends reinvested. This will then help you achieve your objective of tripling your wealth.

However, please be aware, some companies charge a dollar or two a transaction which is reasonable. Some charge five dollars a transaction which is a bit on the steep side, others charge every time a dividend is posted to your account, etc. So be very careful with the DRIP plan. However, they are a good investment vehicle for which to get started with a small amount of money, one-thousand dollars, plus fifty or a hundred dollars per month.

At one point in my life I had four DRIP plans, with McDonalds, Lowes, Exxon and Sears. I felt this represented a fair cross section of retailing, oil and fast foods. However, it is up to you to decide what you want to invest in, oil companies, retail companies, pharmaceutical companies, etc. Truly the decision is up to you. Also, once you get the plans going, you can have the one-hundred a month deducted from your checking account or contribute to it voluntarily as you see fit. In other words, when oil prices are low you might see fit to distribute one or two hundred dollars into the Exxon plan. When retail sales are bad, let us say after a bad winter, you contribute one or two hundred dollars to the DRIP plan for what used to be Sears, which is now Sears Holding, or other retailers such as Lowes.

You might say this takes a lot of time but it really doesn't. Just look at your two or three DRIP plans and decide which one to add the hundred dollars to on a monthly basis. If you feel as if you do not wish to bother deciding every month, I would encourage you to contribute a hundred dollars or fifty dollars to which ever plan you prefer.

However, whatever you do it is wise to look at the statements at least once every six months or once a year and see where you stand. Dividends of course are taxable and you will have to pay Federal and State taxes on the dividends, but these are miniscule.

You will be quite surprised how fast the money multiplies. You will also be quite surprised at the end of the year to see at what prices you bought the stock at.

For example, if you contribute one hundred dollars and Exxon stock is worth fifty dollars you buy two shares. If Exxon stock is sixty-five dollars you only buy 1.5 shares. Conversely, if Exxon stock is twenty-five dollars you buy four shares. Therefore, you are really averaging your investment over time, i.e., sometimes you buy two shares, sometimes you buy one and a half shares, sometimes you buy four shares. This is ideal because no one really knows where the highs and the lows are.

As the investment gets larger you might consider transferring the account, as I have, to my children. Therefore, the dividends and growth, etc. are all attributed to the child's tax return. Child is probably in a lower tax bracket then you will be in the future. Also, the money can be withdrawn for college or other necessities as the child matures.

In addition, should you desire, you can just leave the money in an account under your name and use it for future purchase of a house, car, or other whatever your wishes are in the future. The important point is leaving it in for years.

In summary:

- Amass sum of $1,000.

- Pick out your favorite companies using a Google search engine on the internet, under Google.com.

- Call the companies and find out if they have a DRIP plan (Dividend Reinvestment Plan).

- Get the application and fill it out with the required minimum.

- Try to deposit to it automatically every month. Some require fifty dollars a month, some require a hundred dollars a month.

- You will soon see your wealth increase as you continue to do this.

- If you wish, you can also trade with brokers such as Brown™, E-trade™, and Schwab™. These also usually require one-thousand dollar minimum.

Chapter X

Student Loans

So, you were lucky enough to get a student loan, perhaps a loan combined with a scholarship, GREAT.

Now, you have to pay the loan back.

Do not despair. I have known a Doctor who owed in excess of $200,000 and couldn't get a loan for a home or condominium purchase. I have spoken to many college graduates who owed in excess of $50,000 alone. I, myself, owed money on 3 or 4 student loans.

I asked my uncle what to do and he gave me timeless advice as follows:

1) **Speak to each lender** and ascertain how much you owe, at what interest rate and how many years you have to pay it off.

2) **Ask if there is a deferment allowed.** Sometimes, if you join the service, you can get the amount due lowered proportional to your length of service. Other loaners will defer the amount due for six or nine months until you get a job, etc.

3) Go to other banks and **try to re-finance the entire amount, if possible**.

4) If all else fails, try to **pay off the loan with the highest interest rate first and the loan with the lowest interest rate last.**

5) **Don't** borrow against credit cards as the interest rate approaches 20% and missed payments result in very high fees and also may increase the interest rate automatically.

6) Ask the student loan officer at your school about the possibility of refinancing through a federal agency, eg. Sallie May, Nelllie May, etc.

7) Consider working for non-profits which will credit you $$$$ for years worked. You may make less money, but your loan will be partially paid off when you decide to go to another job.

Chapter XI

Conclusion

I sincerely believe if you follow each one of these steps you will be able to increase your net worth substantially, possibly doubling or tripling your net worth.

Of course, one frequently tends to take shortcuts and by-pass these steps I have defined above. If you do this, do not fret. Just take a step back, take a deep breath and start again.

Many students I have known have rented for years and years. Other students I have known have bought a house immediately upon completing their training. The choice is yours, but a house will probably be your biggest investment in life and should be thought out quite carefully.

Of course to buy a house you need a down payment and this is where the problem lies with many students and ex-students. All of your focus should be on increasing your net worth so as to be able to purchase a house with twenty percent down. Do not buy with zero percent down or five percent down and get stuck with private mortgage insurance. This will lead to increasing debt, increasing monthly payments and increasing financial difficulty. Make sure you have enough, twenty percent for a house.

Should you find that a house in the neighborhood you wish is merely out of sight, unaffordable, cost too much money, etc., please note that you can always by in a suburb next to the town which is too expensive.

For example, houses in Newton and Newton Center run approximately $1 million. I bought a house in Newton Upper Falls which is right next to Newton Center and is considered part of the City of Newton. It has increased in value approximately 3-1/2 times since the time I bought it 10 years ago. Perhaps this is not as much as a home in Newton Center but it still has increased significantly.

In summary, I wish you all the best of luck and remember "a penny saved is a penny earned" or in today's logo, "three dollars not spent at Starbucks™ is three dollars earned tax free".